Spider Life

By Leslie Dinaberg

The
Child's
World®
www.childsworld.com

Published in the United States of America by The Child's World®
P.O. Box 326 • Chanhassen, MN 55317-0326
800-599-READ • www.childsworld.com

Special thanks to my son, Koss, a budding spider scientist.

ACKNOWLEDGMENTS

The Child's World®: Mary Berendes, Publishing Director

Produced by Shoreline Publishing Group LLC
President / Editorial Director: James Buckley, Jr.
Designer: Tom Carling, carlingdesign.com
Cover Art: Slimfilms
Copy Editor: Beth Adelman

Photo Credits
Cover—Main: Dreamstime.com; iStock (other three)
Interior—Corbis: 7, 8, 10, 12 (bottom), 25; iStock: 17, 20, 21, 26, 28;
Minden Pictures: 12 (top); Natural History Museum: 11;
Photos.com: 4, 6, 13, 18;

LIBRARY OF CONGRESS CATALOGING-IN-PUBLICATION DATA

Dinaberg, Leslie.
  Spider life / by Leslie Dinaberg.
    p. cm. — (Boys rock!)
  Includes bibliographical references and index.
  ISBN 1-59296-737-X (library bound : alk. paper)
  1. Spiders—Juvenile literature. I. Title. II. Series.
  QL458.4.D56 2006
  595.4'4—dc22
                              2006002313

CONTENTS

MEET THE
Spinners

Spiders have been spinning webs on Earth since the time of the dinosaurs. Today, there are billions of spiders in the world. Scientists have found more than 37,000 different types of spiders.

Insects have six legs, but spiders have eight. Spiders belong to a group of animals called **arachnids**. Arachnids were named after Arachne (uh-RACK-nee), a character in ancient Greek stories. Arachne was such an expert weaver that she beat the goddess Athena in a contest. Athena was so jealous that she turned Arachne into a spider who weaved forever.

Drops of dew outline the delicate beauty of this spider's carefully woven web.

Spiders have eight eyes! On this close-up view of a jumping spider, you can see four shiny round eyes on the front of its head.

Different types of spiders have different ways of moving—and different ways of hunting, too. Jumping spiders can leap 40 times their body length. They hunt insects by **pouncing**, the way cats hunt mice. Spitting spiders move very slowly.

They catch speedy flies by spitting out a net of poison and glue. Fishing spiders eat the insects that live around freshwater streams and ponds. They dive into the water to catch bugs for dinner. They even catch and eat small fish!

This fishing spider has caught a dragonfly and is enjoying a nice lunch!

Spiders such as this house spider use their eight legs to walk over any sort of ground. Their feet have tiny claws that help them cling to almost any surface.

Spiders use their eight legs with ease. To see what it might be like, try walking like a spider does. Stand back-to-back with three friends, link your arms, and try to walk across the room. Eight legs need a lot of control!

Spider Strength!

The strongest humans can lift five or six times their body weight. A spider can lift 170 times its body weight! If you were that strong, you'd be able to lift more than 10,000 pounds (4,536 kg)! You could easily pick up a car.

The speediest spider in the world is the giant house spider. This fairly common **species** can run 330 times its own body length in 10 seconds. To give you an idea of how fast that is, people can only run 50 times their body length in 10 seconds. So while you can outrun a spider, most insects can't.

Scientists divide animals into different species based on the animals' body type and other things.

Insects have three main body parts. On the other hand, spiders only have two body parts. Their head and **thorax** are combined into one part, which is where their legs attach. Their other body part is their abdomen.

The world's biggest spider is the goliath bird-eating spider, which lives in the jungles of South America. The biggest goliath spider ever found measured more than 11 inches (28 cm) across—bigger than this book! The world's smallest

How does a spider catch a bird? The same way it catches insects—in a web. Plus, in this case, the birds are small . . . and the spider is really big!

spider is the Samoan moss spider, which lives on the island of Samoa. This spider is so small that it would fit on the period at the end of this sentence.

Yikes! This is the actual size of the goliath bird-eating spider. Now, aren't you glad you're not a bird?

Some people find spiders so scary that fear of spiders has a special name. A fear is called a *phobia*.

Spider-Man!

The Spider-Man comic books (from Marvel Comics) and movies tell the story of Peter Parker, an ordinary man bitten by a radioactive spider. The bite gives him incredible strength, "spider" sense, and the ability to climb walls and ceilings. Spider-Man first appeared in a comic book in 1962.

Arachnaphobia is a fear of arachnids. Eek!

Most spider bites don't really hurt humans. In fact, if a spider bites you, you might not even feel it. Spider bites always leave two holes in the skin, from the spider's toothlike **fangs**.

Another close-up look at a spider. Check out the pair of fangs on the front of its head!

Spiders might not be harmful to humans, but they're a big threat to many kinds of insects.

2

WEAVING WEBS OF
Wonder

14

Spiders use their bodies to make a fine thread called *silk*. Some insects, such as silkworms and some moths, can make silk only at certain times. Spiders can make silk all the time. In fact, they can make a new web every day. Most spiders use their webs to trap food.

Some species of spiders recycle! When webs made by these spiders get old, they don't just throw away the silk. Instead, they eat it! They turn the old silk into new silk to make a new web.

OPPOSITE PAGE
Delicate but strong: Most spiderwebs have small strands that connect longer strands going outward from the center.

15

Spider silk is incredibly strong. If you made a steel thread the same thickness as spider silk, the silk would be three times stronger. To make the web, a spider squeezes out a liquid, sort of like toothpaste coming out of a tube. The liquid hardens when it comes in contact with air.

Each spider species makes its own kind of web. Baby spiders don't have to learn how to make them—they are born with that knowledge.

Spiders live in just about every habitat on Earth (except the ocean). They live in forests, in caves, on mountains, in trees . . . just about everywhere.

The silk made by Australia's golden **orb** weaver is the strongest natural fiber we know of. In fact, this spider's webs are so strong, people use them for fishing nets!

Sometimes we see tiny spiders floating through the air, as if they can fly. They can't really fly—instead, they're blown by the wind. They use their silk threads like tiny parachutes, traveling with the wind for hundreds of miles. Scientists called this *ballooning*.

To launch into the air, a spider climbs to a high point and turns to face the wind. It shoots out several strands of silk that are carried up into the air. The spider stands on tiptoe. When the air blows

hard enough, the spider
lets go and floats away on
the breeze.

Up, up, and
away . . . as
the sun sets,
this spider
sets sail for a
short trip.

Spiders lay hundreds of eggs at one time. They use their web-spinning skills to help protect the eggs before they hatch. Orb weaver spiders put their eggs in a little **sac** made of silk. Black widow spiders go a step farther— they glue their egg sacs to tree branches.

Some spiders use silk to make bags, or sacs, to hold their eggs.

Look closely and you can see a baby spider following its mother on a web.

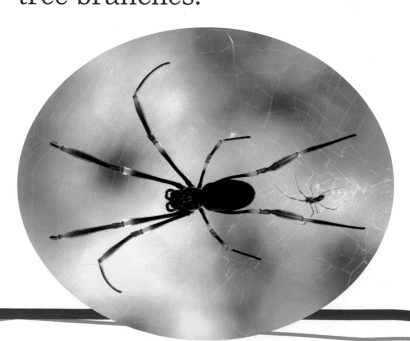

Little Miss Muffet

Do you remember how Little Miss Muffet sat on a tuffet in the famous nursery rhyme? Well, Patience Muffet was a real little girl in the 1500s. Her father, the Reverend Thomas Muffet, was a spider expert. Like many people of that time, he falsely believed that eating mashed spiders could cure many diseases, including the common cold. No wonder she was scared of spiders!

When some types of baby spiders are born, they have nothing to eat but each other, until they are big enough to build their own webs. Only about 25 of every 100 baby spiders survive.

FRIENDS AND Enemies

Although most spiders are harmless to humans, a few can be dangerous. For instance, a single bite from a female black widow spider can kill a person. Luckily, black widows hide from people most of the time and bite only if they're disturbed.

If a big insect or scorpion gets stuck in its web, all the black widow has to do is bite, stand back, and *wham!*—dinner is served. There is also a perfectly harmless spider called the false black widow that looks just like the deadly black widow. It has no red patch on its underside, though.

See that red mark on this black widow spider? If you see that on a spider, stay away!

The deadliest spiders in the world are Brazilian wandering spiders. These spiders don't spin webs. Instead, they wander the jungle floor searching for food. They also enter peoples' homes and hide in their shoes and clothes! They produce a strong poison, or **venom**, and they're quick to attack.

The Australian funnel-web spider is among the world's deadliest. Although its bite can make humans sick, its venom doesn't harm dogs!

Some snakes are venomous, too. Like spiders, they use their fangs to shoot venom into animals they bite.

What about tarantulas?
You've probably seen these
hairy spiders on television
or in movies. Their bites
hurt, but tarantulas aren't
as deadly as most people
think. In fact, they can make
very nice pets!

*This Brazilian
wandering
spider has
caught an
insect for
its dinner.*

This zebra spider has caught and bitten an insect and is wrapping it in silk.

Most spiders use their toothlike fangs to shoot venom into the animals. The venom kills the animals or makes them unable to move.

The spiders also shoot juices into the animals' bodies that turn the insides to liquid, which the spider sucks out. The hard outer coverings of most insects are often too tough for spiders to break down. Instead, the coverings are simply thrown away.

Sometimes a spider catches an insect but doesn't kill and eat it right away. Instead, it wraps the captured insect in silk and saves it for later. Then it can be sure of a nice fresh meal whenever it feels hungry again. It's sort of like a spider kitchen.

The next time you see a spiderweb, look for little balls of webbing. Inside, you might see insects that are a future spider meal.

This pink crab spider shows how some spiders use color to blend in.

Spiders play an important role in the delicate balance of nature. Their eating habits may be one reason they have been around as long as they have.

The Spider Dance

In Taranto, Italy, about 600 years ago, people believed that dancing was the only cure for a poisonous spider's bite. The town gave its name to the tarantula spider and also to a dance called *tarantella*, which became very popular in the United States.

Spiders will eat almost any kind of insect (among other things!) they can catch—and they catch a lot!

Most species of spiders should be welcome in any garden or home. They help keep your house, your food, and your garden free from bugs.

GLOSSARY

arachnids the family of animals that includes spiders

fangs teeth or pointed body parts that stick out from the face or mouth

orb another word for a sphere, or a ball shape

pouncing jumping on top of another animal, especially while hunting

sac a little bag

species one type of animal or plant

thorax name for an insect's midsection

venom a poison some animals make in their bodies

FIND OUT MORE

BOOKS

Amazing Spiders
by Alexandra Parsons
(Alfred A. Knopf, New York) 1990
It's a close-up look at some cool members of the spider family.

Deadly Spiders and Scorpions
by Andrew Solway
(Heinemann Library, Chicago) 2004
Look for photos and fun facts about tarantulas, black widows, and other fascinating spiders.

Spiders
by Seymour Simon
(HarperCollins, New York) 2003
Explores how spiders make their webs, what they eat, how many eyes they have, which spiders are poisonous, and more.

Spinning Spiders
by Melvin Berger
(HarperTrophy, New York) 2000
Spiderwebs are the focus of this book on arachnids.

WEB SITES

Visit our home page for lots of links about spiders:
www.childsworld.com/links

Note to Parents, Teachers, and Librarians: We routinely check our Web links to make sure they're safe, active sites—so encourage your readers to check them out!

INDEX

LESLIE DINABERG has more than 14 years of experience as a writer and editor for several magazines, Web sites, and newspapers. She has written countless articles on subjects ranging from tractors to lions, surfing, and video games, but this is the first time she has written on arachnids since her fourth-grade book report on *Charlotte's Web*.